EXIT STRATEGY

HOW TO GO FROM WHERE YOU ARE NOW TO WHERE YOU DESIRE TO BE

IN 90 DAYS

A Simple Strategy Anyone Can Use In Any Area Of Life

Author:
LaQuita Sharee Lewis-Poole

Exit
Strategy

LaQuita Sharee Lewis-Poole

Copyright © 2015 by LaQuita Sharee Lewis-Poole
Published by LSL Media & Publishing
Oklahoma City, Oklahoma 73141
ISBN: 13: 978-0692410257
ISBN: 10: 0692410252

LSLP Global Empowerment
820 South MacArthur Blvd Ste 105-240
Coppell, TX 75019
www.laquitapoole.com

Ordering Information:
Quantity sales. Special discounts are available on quantity purchases by corporations, associations, and others. For details, contact the publisher at the address above.

"How Exit Strategy Began"

For years I have wanted more from life. I was always trying to figure out ways to get ahead of where my current situation was. I was never content with the normal as my peers were. I always wanted more. I dreamed of more every day. When my life was at its best, I still wanted more. I wanted to do more, I wanted to give more, I wanted to plant more seeds and help more people. As life went on, and I was faced with painful situations and life-changing lessons, I learned that in order to have more and be more, I needed to do things differently than those around me.

I started planning ways to get away from the struggle I had known most of my life. I would pretend I was a very important celebrity that had all the money, success and happiness in the world, and that nothing would be impossible for me if I would just try.

Soon after graduating college I started looking into starting a business. I had no idea what I was going to do, but I had a million ideas run through my head daily. At the time I was working, and I mean working hard. From the time I was pregnant with my first child, I began working two jobs while attending college full time. It was hard, but I had every intention to give my child something I never had. This is also when I realized that I was a fighter, because when everyone thought I should give up, I kept pushing my way through.

When I first started working on my own, I worked as a contractor for the state of Oklahoma as a Behavioral Health Rehabilitation Specialist. It was my first job being self-employed. I absolutely loved it! Being self-employed was exactly what I needed for the sake of my very ill son at the time. I made my own hours and never had to ask to take off when I needed to be a mommy to my baby boy. After being self-employed for over a year, I realized I could never go back to the corporate world. I continued working two jobs to support the lifestyle I wanted to live for me and my son. I left the corporate world for good back in 2006 and began to only do self-employed contract work for the next two years.

In October of 2008, I started my very own business. It was a non-profit organization for teen mothers. As I stated earlier I have always wanted to help others and through all of my work experience with teenagers, from being a substitute teacher to a juvenile officer and then a case worker for the state, I had found a new passion.

As a case worker for the state of Oklahoma, I had dealt with many teen moms and finding placements for them after they aged out of the system. After doing much research into homes for teen mothers, I found there was a huge need for more. My first quest began with wanting to start a home for first-time teen mothers and their children.

So for two years after leaving the corporate world I began some serious planning, investigating and research on how to start a group home for teen mothers. After much research on the cost of such an endeavor and realizing that I didn't have thousands of dollars to invest, I began to think of ways to work with teen mothers without housing them, thus Teen Mothers Second Chance, INC. was created. I was super excited that I had taken a dream of mine from a dream to reality. I had no idea how to get grants for funding nor did I know much of how to start a business, but I wanted it so bad that I learned what I needed to along the way.

I was so dedicated to my dream that I started a third job just to acquire enough independent funding. Yes, people said that I was crazy, but I did it anyway. The look on the young mother's faces, when I was able to help them, was worth more than the restlessness, tiredness or money to me. I made no excuses. I was determined to help as many of them as I could.

In November of 2010, my oldest son began having terrible migraines. They were so bad that the doctors recommended home school due to him missing classes so often. This situation caused me to have to pull back a little to care for my son. However, I kept pushing and helping as many teen mothers as I could.

In January of 2011, my youngest son was hospitalized four times in a week with an unknown bout of illness that nearly took his life. This was the turn of everything for me. It was in January of 2011 that I closed the teen program and quit one of my jobs to focus on homeschooling both of my children.

In April of 2011, I began my first company as an Limited Liability Company. With all the knowledge I had acquired from being a company president, mentor, family advocate, detention officer, case worker, therapist(us), case manager and behavioral health rehabilitation specialist I was ready to start my own counseling agency.

By June of 2011, I had acquired a nationally recognized Commission on Accreditation of Rehabilitation Facilities and prepared all the paperwork and plans to start a counseling agency. At this time in my life, I knew exactly who I was, what I was capable of and what I wanted for me and my children's lives. I had been using a certain strategy to get where I wanted to go every time I made a big shift in my life. Never once complaining about how hard it was or how much work I had to do to get there. It was natural for the entrepreneurial soul inside of me. I wanted my hard work to pay off, but I also wanted to enjoy what I was doing to the fullest.

After running the counseling business for about a year and a half, I began to have that urge to want more and to be able to give more again. It wasn't about the money, I didn't quite like working behind a desk 60-70 hours a week. I honestly didn't like depending on the money I was making from the state to fund my dream and the life I wanted to lead. I was looking for a way to be more, do more and give more, all while enjoying the process more.

Realizing by this time I had already started 4 different businesses, from wedding planning to clothing design, it was time to invest myself in something that I could do for the rest of my life. I had always loved speaking and giving advice to others based on my life experiences, and had always dreamed of finding the perfect outlet to do so. After much research, I came across Life Coaching. This is when my life truly changed.

After becoming dual Certified as a Professional Life Coach and Youth & Family Coach in January of 2013, I began a journey that has not only changed my life but the lives of those around me. I first set a date to close the counseling agency because I was no longer happy with that type of work. The more I learned about coaching I could not ask for a better fit for my life. The love I have for helping others turn their dreams into reality, grows greater each time I coach a client.

Over the past three years, I have invested more into my life than I could have ever imagined: from coaches and mentors, classes, personal development books and attending seminars and conferences. It has been the most rewarding time of my life.

After years of doing it the best way I knew how: putting in the long hours and hard work required to make my dreams a reality, one of the most powerful things I found was that the most successful people had a dream and a strategy to get there.

Exit Strategy

For years I had been using journals, pens and pads to plot out my future and my goals. The more I did this, the more it became part of my daily routine. I never knew that having a predetermined plan on paper was helping me turn my visions into a reality. I was doing something so early in my life that actually got me so much further ahead than just having thoughts run around in my head. In my experience, writing things out, making a plan and looking at it daily pushed me to get things done despite the obstacles.

Exit Strategy was born when a friend and colleague of mine called to ask for advice about her situation of working in Corporate America while trying to work towards her dream at the same time. I began to tell her how I had plans on leaving my job as a contractor because it was taking away from me doing the things I wanted to do in my own business. As the conversation continued, I told her to give herself 90 days to save and plan to leave her job and go full time in her own business. Naturally, 90 days seems like such a long time for someone who has already started their own business and have experienced what it's like to work for yourself.

Therefore, while 90 days is right for some, it may only take another person 60 days to complete the process of making sure they have the basics in place before leaving their day job.

A few weeks later I received a call from that friend to update me on her progress. She told me that she just got up and quit her job one day. She explained to me why she did it, and I told her that when you have a gut feeling about anything, you follow it. And that as an entrepreneur you sometimes have to make tough decisions in the face of uncertainty, but that is what separates the leaders from the followers. When you take on a leadership role, you will be faced with making tough decisions. If you fall, get back up and do it again until you accomplish what you set out to do.

We discussed how the strategy I had always used to make positive movements in my own life could help others who are stuck trying to figure out where they need to go in business and in life. We strategized together and thus the Exit Strategy was born.

LaQuita Sharee Lewis-Poole

EXIT STRATEGY
CONTENTS

ACKNOWLEDGMENTS

First, I want to thank God for this journey I am on.

To my sons, Jordon and Shemar: Without you by my side life would have been pointless, at times, in my eyes. Jordon you have been my angel since I gave birth to you. You have been my rock when all we had was each other. Thank you son for believing in me even when I had times I didn't think I was going to make it. You reached back and gave me the same love and encouragement I have always given you. I love you Jordon!
Shemar you are the light to my world. When mommy was down you always made me smile. In good and bad times you were the one who brightened my world with your smile. I love you Shemar! You both are my reasons for becoming fearless and unstoppable.

To my husband, Glendon: Thank you for your love and support.

To my grandparents: Carl and Delores Boone, my biggest fans from early childhood until their passing, I love you both with all of my heart and soul. Thank you for believing in my abilities and my future before I believed in myself. Thank you for raising me to be a "go getter" at everything I set my mind to. You may be gone but the love, time and care you gave me will never be forgotten. Rest in peace!

To my mother, Nancy: Thank you for giving me life and being my mother.

To my brothers and sister, Robert, Tyree and TaMeca: Thank you for loving me and supporting me through it all.

To all those who have supported me, I want to thank you from the bottom of my heart for believing in me.

To You: Thank you for purchasing this book and allowing me to assist you in making your dreams a reality.

INTRODUCTION

You're ready to move from where you are currently to where you desire to be. All real change starts with a plan or strategy. Before anything takes place in your life, you must think about it first. To move from one place to another successfully, you need a strategy. To go from one relationship to another, you need a strategy. To go from Single to Married, you need a strategy. Nothing in life is done without a Strategy. Even if you just get up and go do something that was not planned you have a strategy behind it. The strategy is essential.

In this guide, you will learn how to use a simple strategy to take you from where you are currently to where you desire to be. You can use this simple formula to start your own business or you can use parts of this formula to help you go from one relationship to the next, go from being single to married or even move clear across the country. It was designed for entrepreneurs, but many parts of this strategy can be used in your own personal life as well. The strategy was designed for entrepreneurs or those aspiring to have their own business and go from working for someone else to working for themselves. The basics of this strategy are to simply know who you are and what it is that you want and put a strategy in place to get it.

There is no magic to this. If you can follow the steps in this Exit Strategy guide, be willing to put in the work, hold yourself accountable and stay true to your own desires for your life, in no time you will be looking back and saying, "Wow, I did it."

Your exit strategy begins now.

EXIT STRATEGY

This way

PHASE ONE (PREPARE)

COMPLETE THIS FIRST PHASE DAYS 1-30

WHAT DO I WANT?

Knowing why you are here and what you are here for is an essential first step in any process of change. What is your divine assignment? What end result are you seeking? What makes you completely happy? Whatever your divine purpose is will allow you to live the life you have been dreaming of.

Many people tend to do things and work jobs that are unsatisfying, working day to day, week to week and year to year just to make ends meet. The real satisfaction comes from finding out what it is you truly desire to do and following the path that will allow you to do just that.

In order to do this, you must be very clear about exactly what it is you want. Clarity is key in the initial phase. You do not want to find yourself years into a business where you end up burnt-out or uninspired. People who have done that are not sure what their divine assignment is. And that's ok.

A divine assignment is different than a purpose. Your purpose on the road to your destiny will change along the journey, but your ultimate goal, your divine assignment will always be the same. So get crystal clear about what it is that's deep down inside your heart. You have a calling and a purpose each and every second of each and every day that you are alive. Get clear about what that is.

Without clarity, there can be no progress. In order to get clear, you must take some time out and dig deep within yourself to find what it is that only you were created to do in this earth. Some may already know but for others it may take some time to brainstorm and really focus on your likes and dislikes, what you want to accomplish in life or what legacy would you like to leave behind.

Before moving forward complete the following questions in as much detail as possible. Be totally honest with yourself and do not limit yourself. Anything you can dream you can achieve.

*What is my divine assignment?

_____
_____
_____
_____
_____
_____
_____

_____
_____
_____
_____

*Make a list of all your desires and dreams below:

_____
_____
_____
_____
_____
_____
_____
_____
_____
_____
_____
_____

*What is my purpose right now? You could have more than one purpose. List them below:

_____
_____
_____
_____
_____
_____
_____
_____
_____
_____
_____
_____
_____

{Life Lesson}

I first completed this exercise during my training to become a life coach. At first I listed all of the things I've always wanted in life. You know, the list that you tell your close friends frequently enough. I wanted all the money in the world, to be able to travel without having to worry about going to work, to buy the big house and have my choice of vehicles.

Most of us want what we feel we can't have. However, I've learned that, in reality, you can have everything your heart desires, but you must believe you are worthy of receiving it and then know it's purpose. Then you dedicate yourself towards accomplishing that; which you truly desire.

By the end of the second week of my life coach training, I realized that my divine assignment was key to the success and abundance that I truly desired for my life. I learned that when you get to the core of who you really are and the legacy you want to leave behind for your children and family, you have found the success your heart truly desires.

My coach taught me that true abundance comes from living your life the way it was intended for you from the beginning. You are not meant to live in deprivation, in fear, anxiety, and/or working a job that is draining you or unsatisfying.

I learned that as you give your gift and love back to the world, the world will gift you with the desires of your heart. Then, and only then, can you live the life you so desire for yourself and create the legacy you desire to leave behind.

WHY DO I WANT THIS?

Many people have dreams and desires that they never accomplish in life because they have no idea why they want those dreams or desires for themselves. When you have no idea why you want something, you can't appreciate the process. Therefore, you may never fully activate what God has already blessed you to have. In order to accomplish those dreams and desires for yourself, you must have a strong why.

Having a strong why means that you have connected your dreams and goals to something of value or purpose. Your strong why will help you remain focused, dedicated and committed to you accomplishing that which you say you want. While being motivated by your family, friends, a mentor or coach is awesome, your why has to be what makes you get up every morning lit up and ready to put in the hours, the hard work and dedication needed to make your dreams come true.

Below are some questions to assist you in finding your strong why:

*What is my why for what it is that I am seeking?

_____
_____
_____
_____
_____
_____
_____
_____

*Is my why so strong that it will motivate me when I am facing adversity, obstacles and even when I feel like giving up?

_____
_____
_____
_____
_____
_____

{Life Lesson}

All of my life I have wanted to be successful and to show my family that I could do anything I wanted regardless of the odds against me.

My grandparents were always very supportive of my crazy ideas and dreams as a child. They would always tell me that I was going to do great things in this world. At that time I had no idea what they were talking about, but the feeling it gave me to know I would be great someday helped me stay focused and committed to any number of aspirations I had growing up.

As a child, I knew that no matter what I did my grandparents were always going to be there to support me. This was the beginning of me finding my why for the things I did in life. For years, I dreamed, I wrote, I pretended, and I told my closest friends the things I would accomplish one day. And the only reason I knew I would at that time was because my grandparents told me over and over I would be successful and live a wonderful life.

As the years went by, I got older and had a child of my own. I went to college and though my dreams and desires changed, I knew the plan was to keep pushing until I had the success that I desired. After having my son, the desire of my heart was to give him everything he deserves to live a complete and full life and to make sure he knew he could be and do anything he dreamt of if he stayed committed to the process. He was my reason why at this stage of my life.

As life continued, I had many different reasons why I needed to keep pushing myself to get to the next level, as we all do. Every stage of life brings a different process and a different struggle that we have to be able to get through to get to the next level. If your why is not strong enough to keep you going, you will fail.

VISUALIZE

You already have everything you desire right now. Close your eyes and see yourself as the successful CEO, the director, the owner or the president of your company. Don't wait for approval from others. When you have a strong desire or big dream inside of you, go for it in your mind first. If you can get your mind to believe what your heart desires, it will become your reality in a matter of time.

Visualizing the life you want to live now will create opportunities for you to live that life in the near future. Our thoughts become the very things we get in life. This is why it is so important to watch the way in which you speak about yourself, your future and others. Every thought you carry in your mind will manifest itself right before your eyes. So it is quite obvious that you would want to create positive thoughts and feelings intentionally every second of the day.

This entire process only works when you can visualize your dream and then put yourself in the desired situation in that very moment. Feel yourself running the business, making the money, taking the vacation and so forth. So take at least 15 minutes or more a day and just sit in a quiet room or place where you feel relaxed, close your eyes and let your mind go beyond where your reality currently is.

Feeling what your desires are while you are visualizing them will allow them to manifest much faster. You can't just visualize making a million dollars. You need to feel yourself receiving the million dollars and then feel yourself spending it on your desires. Feeling is just as important as visualizing your dreams and desires.

Here is a great assignment you can do to assist you with visualizing:

*Create a vision board, book or wall and fill it with all the things you want to create for yourself in the future. Then visit the vision board daily and feel yourself with those things right now. Use your imagination to the fullest.

Live it, smell it, feel it! Know that you can have anything you desire.

{Life Lesson}

When I was first told to create a vision board by my coach, I didn't feel like I really needed it. I had been seeing myself as successful for many, many years, and I knew it was going to happen for me. But when I began to do the exercise I not only visualized my dreams coming true but I felt the things I desired most in my heart being mine.

I learned that creating a vision board or wall is not just about putting up some pictures of things you have always wanted but it's about making those things you desire most have meaning and become real in your mind first before you actually receive them. As I completed the exercise, I found myself being grateful that I had the ability to obtain the things I desired and dreamed of.

A vision board, wall or a book is something you should use and look at every day. It needs to be in a place where you can see it when you need encouragement or just a simple reminder of why you're on this phenomenal journey.

BELIEVING

Do you believe in you? Do you believe that you deserve the desires of your heart? Do you believe that you can live a full life of happiness, joy, love and abundance?

You must believe in yourself and your abilities for change to come about in your life. If you are half way in and half way out you will not accomplish your goals or the desires of your heart. Your mind has to believe and receive your desires before they can become your reality.

You need to have unshakable confidence in the power God has given you. Everything you need to get your dreams and desires to come into reality is already inside you. The 90-day Exit Strategy is just a tool to help you unleash the power that is lying dormant in your life and make use of resources that are available to assist you in accomplishing those tasks.

You must learn to believe in yourself even when you have no one else cheering you on. It's hard to play on a team with no support. So if you have it, appreciate it. If you do not have support become your own biggest fan and you will soon have people cheering you on.

Start writing and saying powerful belief statements about yourself daily to help encourage and boost your self-confidence. Example: "I live with the power of God flowing through me daily."

Take some time and ask yourself the following questions and be honest with yourself:

*What do I believe about myself?

_____
_____
_____
_____
_____
_____
_____
_____
_____
_____
_____

*What am I worthy of?

_____
_____
_____
_____
_____
_____

*Write down several powerful belief statements about yourself and repeat daily to help you increase belief in yourself. Example: I am powerful, and I am accomplishing my dreams. All statements should be in the present tense.

1.

_____
_____
_____

2.

_____
_____
_____

3.

_____
_____
_____

4.

_____
_____
_____

5.

_____
_____
_____

6.

_____
_____
_____

7.

_____
_____
_____

8.

_____
_____
_____

9.

_____
_____
_____

10.

_____
_____
_____

11.

_____
_____
_____

12.

_____
_____
_____

13.

_____
_____
_____

14.

_____
_____
_____

{Life Lesson}

One of the hardest things to do in life is to give yourself the credit you truly deserve. For years I planned, I put together, I created, I accomplished, I kept pushing through and I didn't give up on the desires of my heart. I don't remember ever having someone believe in me as much as I believe in myself today.

My grandmother was my angel, and as she raised me I knew she believed in me with all of her heart. As a child and a teenager, I didn't understand how or why she believed so much in me that no matter what I did or didn't do, she never gave up on me.

It took me years to develop the type of confidence I have in myself today. It took failing over and over again only to get up and keep trying before I realized that I have to start believing in myself. While my grandmother believing in all my dreams and visions was what gave me my drive to do the things I wanted to do in life, I realized she would not always be around to express that to me.

My grandmother; best friend, advisor, mentor and angel passed away April of 2006. I didn't start my first business until October of 2008. For two years, I had to learn to believe in myself the way she believed in me all of my life. It didn't happen overnight but as the days, and months went by I wanted to make her proud. So I learned to use the tools she gave me, the bible, prayer, and my instinct, to increase belief in my abilities.

I am becoming everything I've ever wanted to be and more. I now know that everything means nothing if you don't believe in yourself first.

GRATITUDE

One of the fastest ways to see your dreams and desires come into reality is to be grateful for where you are right now in this very moment. When you give thanks for all the things you have already been blessed to receive, you receive more.

It is often hard to feel gratitude for all that we have because we began to take things for granted. If you would just stop and slow down for a moment to show gratitude for all the things you have, don't have, and the things that you desire; all of what you want will come to you much faster.

Your job is to trust the process no matter how tough, how easy or how many obstacles you face on this journey. Everything in your life you have had to face was part of your journey. If anything in your life, good or bad, would have been different you would not be who you are today. You have a divine assignment to fulfill.

Practice being grateful for all things including those things you are waiting for. Being in a constant state of gratitude allows your frequency (energy) to vibrate at a higher level. This process will allow you to bring into existence the things you desire even faster.

While you are expressing gratitude, do it from your heart. Don't just say you're grateful, but truly feel the gratitude in every thought and each step you take daily. This process is life changing when done from the heart each and every day.

Here are some simple ways to show gratitude:

*Keep a gratitude journal and write in it daily.

*Take at least 10 minutes per day to express your gratitude.

*Write gratitude letters to those who you appreciate and are grateful to have in your life.

*Cheerfully give away a dollar or more a day to a stranger.

{Life Lesson}

I learned over a year ago how much showing gratitude can really make a difference in your life. At first it seemed like doing an exercise to show gratitude was silly. After reading more on gratitude from the book, The Secret, I realized just how much showing gratitude each and every day is important to the process of getting exactly what it is that you want.

I remember growing up, my grandparents would always tell me to be grateful for everything in my life. What they didn't tell me is that showing heartfelt gratitude for everything you have now will increase what you have tomorrow.

Many people grow up with the thinking that you are to only be grateful for the good things in your life. The truth is that you need to be grateful for all things in your life. The good, bad and everything in between. Everything you grow through in life is there for a purpose. It could be to push you into your destiny, it could be to keep you from going down the wrong path or it could be that you are going through something's in life as an example for someone else. This is why you need to be grateful for all the things in your life at all times.

I keep a gratitude journal that I write in daily. You can start with something as simple as getting up every morning and stating to yourself the things you are grateful for and then again before you go to bed each night.

Always show gratitude for the things you have now and the things you desire to have in your future. Your life will become infinitely richer.

INVEST

Exit Strategy

In order to exit from one stage, level or place in your life, there must be some level of investment involved. You cannot go from poor to rich without putting in an investment. You cannot go from high school to college without some form of investment. You cannot go from a 9-5 to running a successful company without investing in yourself and your business. Absolutely nothing in life worth having is free. There will always be some type of investment involved.

If you have never invested in yourself today is a great day to start. You invested in this book to learn new skills or information you otherwise would not have known. As you follow along in this book, there will be many things you will be advised to invest in to progress towards your ambitions.

So many people want to run a successful business, but they don't want to invest what it will take to acquire the knowledge or information needed in order to do so. Remember the more you put into yourself, your business or anything you do in life, the more you will get out of it.

As you become successful and begin to make hundreds, thousands or millions of dollars, your investments will become greater as well. So be prepared to always put an investment in to get something out. This is not a time to hold back.

Investments could include any of the following:

*Your time
*Monetary funds
*Taking classes to sharpen your skills
*Networking with others who may be able to assist you
*Reading books on your subject or interest
*Hiring a Coach or Mentor

Start investing in yourself and your business as soon as you know you want to be a successful business owner or make a change in your personal life. It is never too early to set money aside to start your own company or plan for your future desires. You have 90 days to invest as much as you can so when it is time to move forward no excuses are allowed.

{Life Lesson}

In 2008 when I started my first non-profit business I had no idea that funding would be so hard to come by as a new business owner. I did not want to go into debt trying to accomplish a dream, so I stayed away from applying for business loans. After completing my business plan and getting some great financial advice from other nonprofits, I decided to pick up an additional job to fund my dream.

It wasn't easy at first because I was already working two jobs and going to school. My desire to be successful was so strong that I did what was necessary to see my vision come to reality.

I worked three jobs while completing my Master's degree and raising two sons as a single mother. I do not believe in excuses when there is opportunity all around. You may have to do some extra work, put in some extra hours and give up a lot of the extracurricular activities in your life to accomplish your dreams, but it will be worth it in the end.

I invested knowledge, time, energy and money to make the things I desired come to reality. I get asked by a lot of people how to do it or where to get free assistance. My answer to them is nothing worth having is ever free. Everything you dream of can be funded if you really have the desire to go out and do the work.

Not all dreams require monetary funds to get them going. Some require studying or giving time. Many times you can intern for someone to get the information you need to get started. With all the technology in the world today there is no excuse for anyone with a dream not to get started.

SETTING UP YOUR BUSINESS

Let's get your business set up. There are some things you must do to legally be in business for yourself. Below is an outline and you will have to do some extra work and research with a CPA in order to get your business structure set up for what you will be doing.

Here is an outline to get your business established:

*Choose a name for your business. Do some research to make sure the name is available with your Secretary of State and other outlets you may want to use.

*Set you up a company email address. You can use Google, Yahoo or Hotmail.

*You will need a business address for all your business needs. If you work from home, I suggest you still get a PO Box address so that you keep your home address private from the public.

*Register your business with your state. Make sure you do the research on LLC's, Partnerships, Non-Profit's and Corporations before registering.

*Apply for your EIN, employer identification number, with the IRS. This can be done same day online.

*Open your business bank account. You will need to take your registration papers from the state you registered in as well as have your EIN number handy.

*Register your domain and hosting service. HostGator and Go-Daddy are among the top hosting companies and they come with a business email that you will need for business use.

*Set up your website or have a company or someone else do it for you. Ex. Wix.com or Wordpress.com

*Set up a business PayPal account.

*Set up a business Fiverr account.

This is a basic outline of services and things needed to get you started.

PHASE TWO (MASSIVE ACTION)

COMPLETE THIS SECOND PHASE DAYS 31-60

STAYING
FOCUSED

Exit Strategy

Now it's time to take massive action. You have made it 30 days strong into your Exit Strategy. The skills and tools you have gained thus far will be put into action during this phase. You are ready and equipped to make your dreams happen. Stand up, take a deep breath and get ready to see everything you have been dreaming of begin to come into reality. It's time to get moving.

In this step, it's very important that you remain clear and focused on what's ahead. Live and embrace the present but always being aware of what it is you are creating every moment. During this phase, it will be very important for you to spend some quiet time alone daily for at least 15 minutes and spend time just being quiet and observing your thoughts. Staying positive is an absolute MUST during this entire phase. Stay away from negativity in any form. Surround yourself with only positive people who speak life into you and encourage you to follow your dreams. You always want to surround yourself with people who are where you are trying to go.

This is the phase where you may begin to part way with some friends. When you begin to get deep into making your dreams come true and doing the things that are required of you to complete those tasks, there will be a lot of things you use to do that are no longer going to be a part of your life. Those you started with are not always meant to go with you to the next level. So be really careful who you choose to spend your time with during this very important time of your life.

Becoming a CEO, president or an owner puts you in a different category of people. Not only will you have to stand out from the crowd you will become an example for the people who will eventually follow you. So if you want to be a business owner and you are not ready to be a leader close the book now and give it as a gift to someone you know who is ready to step up to the plate.

It's time to get serious and make those dreams a reality. This is where the leaders are separated from the followers. Are you ready to take on the real challenge?

To help you with this step complete the following questions:

*Do you have a place you can go to that is peaceful for at least 15 minutes per day? If so, where is that place? If not, where is a peaceful place you can go to?

_____
_____
_____
_____
_____
_____
_____

*What is the primary topic of your conversations with the people you interact with daily? Is it negative? If so, how can you change your words and only speak words that are encouraging and positive?

_____
_____
_____
_____
_____
_____
_____

*How many positive relationships do you have that speak life into you and your dreams? If you have none, you need to develop new, supportive friendships.

_____
_____
_____
_____
_____
_____

{Life Lesson}

Before I learned the importance of sitting in silence on a daily basis, I had no idea of the effect it would have on my life. I had heard of doing this before from several coaches and books I had read, but never done it myself. After finally experiencing how beneficial silence is for the mind and body, I began to find the time to make this a routine.

When I first began sitting in silence for 15 minutes, I found it very difficult to stay present. For days as I began to practice this behavior, my mind often wandered and sometimes I even got so relaxed I would doze off for a few minutes. My coach said this was perfectly normal in the beginning.

After about a week or so of practicing for 15 minutes each day and some additional studying on staying present and new ways to relate to a busy mind, I was convinced that this was a practice worth continuing.

As you are learning to observe your thoughts, you learn that you no longer have to be controlled by them. You then have the ability to focus more on positive thoughts and what feels good to you rather than the negative thoughts. Taking the time to sit in silence helps you regain control of who you are and what you do.

Once it becomes a routine for you, you will see a difference in how you handle everyday life. You are likely to be much more relaxed if you take some time each morning, and it's very beneficial to finish out your day as well.

At the end of each day
I always say, "Relax. Reflect. Retry."
~LaQuita Lewis-Poole

BUSINESS PLAN

Exit Strategy

Most people get frustrated when you mention needing a business plan. The truth is without a business plan your business is planning to fail. You must have a well thought out plan of how you will take action in your business from the very beginning. It does not have to be intense and 50 pages long just starting out, but you must have a basic concept/outline of what you are doing. Is it profitable? What your goals are in 1 year, 3 years or even 5 years down the road? Think of it as a road map for your business.

So here are some basics things you need to know and have in your business plan from the very beginning:

*Company Name

*Mission Statement

*Team members

*Market Summary

*Opportunities

*Business Concept

*Competition

*Goals & Objectives

*Financial Plan

*Risk & Rewards

*Key Issues

There are several books on putting together a business plan out there as well as online templates, resources and even companies who will complete your business plan for a fee. Do your research here; having a great business plan is key to a successful business.

{Life Lesson}

I used to read, How to Write a Business Plan for Dummies when I first started out. Check out your local library or Barnes & Noble for business plan books and resources. This is a great start!

You can also find YouTube videos and other information online on how to create a business plan for new business owners. There are many coaches and advisors that have trainings on putting a business plan together on YouTube and other sites. Just do your research to make sure that their credentials are legitimate.

CALENDAR JOURNALING

At the beginning of your 90 Day Exit Strategy it is a good idea to acquire a journal. You will need a calendar journal where you can keep track of appointments, meetings, deadlines and keep up with your timeline and dates. It is always good to use a personal (desk or pocket) calendar so that you can see your progress along the way.

I believe this is one of the most important investments in yourself and business that you can make. Your journal will also be used to set goals and future events for yourself in the future. Planning ahead is always a great idea in business. When purchasing your calendar get a one year calendar so you can plan ahead for the next year as well.

The further you plan ahead the better your life will be. You will give yourself a head start and a firm foundation to stand on when you get side tracked with other things that will inevitably come up. Mark your yearly calendar with important dates for personal and business meetings or occasions. This way you already have it down and can avoid unnecessary double bookings.

Remember these things:

*Make your journal do-able and precise.

*Make a timeline and stick to it, no matter what.

*Set daily goals, weekly goals and monthly goals for yourself and your new business.

*Do exactly what you say you're going to do. Don't deviate from your plans unless absolutely necessary. If you do deviate from your plans, get right back on track.

*Below is just a sample journal I put together as an example of what planning ahead may look like during the 90-day Exit Strategy. This does not include any personal or family events, meetings or occasions.

*Please remember to add your family events to your business calendar to avoid conflicts in time.

*Example Calendar Journal:

Sunday	Monday	Tuesday	Wednesday	Thursday	Friday	Saturday
						1
2 Plan ahead	3 Begin Exit Strategy	4	5	6 Lunch Meeting with Lisa 12pm	7 Review Progress	8 Get Social
9 Plan ahead	10 Net-working	11	12 Networking	13	14 Review Progress	15
16 Plan ahead	17 Meeting 4pm	18	19 Work on Business Plan	20	21 Wrap Up Business Plan/ Review Progress	22 Get Social
23 Plan Ahead	24	25 Strategy Session 3pm	26 Branding Meeting 2pm	27 Branding Meeting 1pm	28 Review Progress	29
30						

BRANDING

Branding is the icing to your business. No business is successful without a strong brand image. This step may require you to hire a branding expert. No worries, there are plenty of them out there. Do not make the mistake of trying to brand yourself if branding is not your forte or passion. Skipping this step is a huge mistake.

You can have a perfect idea, and have it fail because you have not invested in branding the image of your business.

Branding includes having the perfect images and informational pieces to represent your business and your product/service. This can include having the perfect logo, doing photo shoots, having your website designed with your new images, changing your mindset and image to represent who you are, and many other things such as business cards, letter-heads etc. that all match your theme and the image you have set for yourself.

Branding can be fun and should be fun. It is an experience that should help you embrace where you are going and be thankful for how far you have come. With the right branding expert you will get an inside look at a world you will soon come to embrace. This will not be the last time you need a branding expert by your side.

For some branding needs, you can hire companies and individuals online, website's such as Fiverr and Vista-print may be particularly useful for branding services. I suggest you find a branding expert that you can meet with and go over ideas with when it comes to branding yourself. They will need to get a feel for what you like, your personality and how you carry yourself to help you create a fitting brand image.

Answer the following questions to get started:

*What is your brand about?

_____

_____

_____

*Have you researched branding experts in your area or online? If not, get started right away?

_____

_____

_____

{Life Lesson}

I have used several different branding experts at different times throughout my business experience. You may have to work with a few branding experts to find the right one. There are many branding experts out there for you to choose from. When selecting a branding expert, make sure you look for experience, previous customer's reviews, and someone you feel you can develop a good rapport with.

Not every branding expert is a good fit. You want someone who understands your passion and your vision. This is the only way to get the look and feel of your brand. If they try to change your vision to what they think it should be, proceed with caution or not at all.

It's okay to be creative and change concepts and colors, but if your gut is telling you to go with one thing and the branding expert is saying something totally different and you don't quite agree, don't do it.

Remember this is your vision and how you want your business to be represented to the world. So take plenty of time here to think everything through and do the research to find a great branding expert

SOCIAL MEDIA

In the 21ˢᵗ century social media is a must. Social media has become a necessity to any successful business in the modern day. Facebook, Twitter and LinkedIn are among the most popular and widely used social media sites out there.

There are lots of books, resources and trainings out there that will assist and teach you how to incorporate these social media links into your business and create business pages as well. Social Media is also a great platform for you to get business exposure across the US and other countries.

While social media is a great platform for your business, remember it takes work to do it correctly and get the results you are looking for. Social media sites are constantly changing so be prepared to invest in the training for yourself or hire a company or someone to handle this part of your business for you.

Suggested sites to incorporate into your business:

- Facebook Business Page
- Twitter Page
- Google Hangouts
- LinkedIn Profile
- Pinterest (especially for DIY or Fashion)

Be sure to always keep your business and personal social media pages separate as not doing so can be bad for business. You will also need to watch what you share and comment on or to on your personal social media sites. Many business people or potential clients will want to check you out before they do business with you. Remember you are now a professional and need to represent yourself as such.

*Everything matters now. So keep it clean, simple and sweet.

{Life Lesson}

Each social media site has trainings and customer support to help you set up your business page(s). Don't be intimidated by the process because this is something your business needs to be successful.

My Social media links:

www.Facebook.com/laquitathemaven

www.Twitter.com/laquitathemaven

READING

Exit Strategy

Reading motivating, powerful material will enhance your life and your journey. You can only go as far as your mind can grow. One of the most valuable things in life is the ability to read. With all the knowledge that is readily available in the 21st century, there is no excuse to not find some material that will help you on your journey.

You can access any information you need right from the world wide web. Reading expands the mind, increases your vocabulary and opens you up to explore limitless possibilities.

There are many self-made millionaires who started just by reading and doing research online and in books. If you have trouble reading take a reading class or two at a community college or online. Don't let anything keep you from accomplishing your dreams and desires.

If you have a dream or desire to do anything, then it is possible for you to make it a reality. God does not give you a dream or deep desire if he knows you can't fulfill it. So don't be shy or fearful to go get what you deserve.

I've learned so much from reading and studying over the past couple of years. From self-help books to spiritual books. You will be surprised at how much you thought you knew before you took the time to investigate any subject of interest further.

Here are a few of my favorite reads:

*Law of Attraction, The Basics of The Teaching of Abraham by Ester and Jerry Hicks

*Power of Positive Thinking by Norman Vincent Peale

*The Science of Getting Rich by Your Master Key to Success, Wallace D. Wattles

*Think and Grow Rich and The Law of Success by Napoleon Hill

{Life Lesson}

Reading has completely changed my life. My mind has grown in such a tremendous way since I began to take time to embrace the wisdom and knowledge of so many successful people who have come before me.

Reading is the greatest gift of wisdom that a man can give another.

PHASE THREE
(LAUNCH)

*COMPLETE THIS
THIRD PHASE
DAYS 61-90*

BE FEARLESS & UNSTOPPABLE

It's time to shine! There is no room for fear where you are headed. Many people never accomplish their dreams because they fear the unknown. That fear keeps us stuck in the familiar, broke, unhappy and lonely. Break through those fears by continuing to stay focused on the divine assignment and outcome you are creating right now.

This would be a great time to immerse yourself in motivational classes, groups or even finding a coach or mentor to assist you in staying focused and committed regardless of the setbacks and roadblocks you will face. Having that accountability is good if you consistently find yourself falling off the band wagon every time something goes wrong.

Being fearless means to continue forward without fear. Believe in yourself enough to know that whatever you set your mind to, you will succeed. You must be fearless to be successful. There is no room for the weak when you're building a successful business or company.

So many people think they want their own business because they are only looking for money to be made or the benefits of setting their own schedule and working whenever they want. What many people don't realize is when you make the firm and courageous decision to become a business owner you will actually do more work in the beginning than you probably have done in the last year or so at a corporate job. And you may not start making the kinds of money you have dreamed of for a year or more down the line, but you still have to move forward, be consistent and have the faith.

Being unstoppable simply means that until you reach your goals and dreams you will not let anything stop you. Your dreams have to be so real and attainable to you. When you are down you look up and see your dreams and say I must keep going, I have a divine assignment to accomplish. You can't allow obstacles to stop you from achieving that that you wish to have.

I often tell clients that you cannot let a bad hand or a bad situation hold you back from your destiny and dreams. Starting right now take your current situation and replace it with the situation you wish to be in. Keep that in your mind every day from this day forward no matter what. Be unstoppable!

{Life Lesson}

"I became fearless & unstoppable when I realized that I wanted my dreams more than my current reality." ~LaQuita Sharee Lewis-Poole

NETWORKING

This step is so important and necessary for your business and personal success. Without other people, you can't grow. You must start networking as soon as you begin your Exit Strategy.

Find people who are on the same journey as you and then connect with them in some way. Expand your horizons and go beyond the circle of friends you currently have, your community, your state and reach out to groups and communities in other states or even other countries.

Networking can be incredibly powerful. To be surrounded by like-minded people is an awesomely empowering experience. An experience you must have in the business world. So start networking now or continue if you have already begun.

Some places to network are:

*Social Media groups

*Meetup.com

*Eventbrite.com

*Your local Chamber of Commerce

*Groups that cater to your niche/purpose

*Church

*Local events

Groups are really great to be a part of especially if everyone is there to help and support each other. Be careful not to spread yourself too thin across the board because you want to give quality time and make a commitment to be of service to others as much as you need them to be of service to you.

Do not overdue it or over commit yourself. You will regret it later.

{Life Lesson}

As a business owner, I have seen many and had many people ask me how they can become successful in starting their own business. I tell all of them to start connecting with people.

Although you may have the vision and the dream, it will not be accomplished without the assistance of another person or team, big or small. You must be able to connect.

If you do not have people skills, you will need to invest your time in learning how to connect with people. You cannot and will not have a successful business all alone. There is no business owner out there who made it to the top all by themselves.

The assistance of other minds, opinions and reviews is needed for any business to go beyond just a dream and into reality.

Learn to network if you have not already. Start where you are most comfortable, but then venture out and go meet those people who are willing to assist you in making your dream a reality. They are out there waiting.

MARKETING

Exit Strategy

It's time to set a date for your launch event. Give yourself at least 90 days or more to market your event. Now is the time to begin marketing yourself and your business to the world. Your purpose and your vision is no longer a secret. This is your time to put everything you have learned and worked so hard for on the table. Everyone you know that supports you needs to know what you're doing so they can help you spread the word about this exciting time in your life.

Marketing requires you to know who your target audience is. If you have followed along thus far and completed the exercises from the beginning of the book, you should already have a pretty good idea of who you need to be talking to. Knowing what your divine assignment is will sure enough help you pinpoint who you need to be targeting when creating or starting your own business.

You do not want to spend a lot of time and money marketing your business to those not interested in what you have to offer. So be smart and invest some time in pinpointing your target audience right now if you have not done so thus far. Everyone will not need your service or product so be very specific in who you are targeting.

Marketing will also require monetary investments such as ads, flyers, banners, etc. Some people will spend more than others, and some will spend less but this is where you want to invest as much as possible into making sure you are seen everywhere. Not physically everywhere, but all over social media and whatever other types of media you can invest in. You must have an audience in order for your business to be successful. No one will ever know who you are if you do not have a good marketing strategy.

You can hire a company or marketing strategist to do most of your marketing for you if this is not an area you are strong in, but you will still need to be hands on with this project. After all, it is your business and your brand being put out to the world. So be wise in your marketing decision-making and choose someone or a company that understands your message and brand.

{Life Lesson}

I learned marketing the hard way. When I started my first business, I had no trainings in marketing, and I did whatever I thought I needed to do to get my business in front of the public eye. At the time Facebook was not as popular as it is today, so I did what a lot of older business had to do, cold calling, posting fliers and going to businesses to talk with the directors or owners about myself and my business.

Needless to say, I am glad I got the experience because I know now that I can use social media as well as personal contact to market my business. You can opt to hire a Marketing company to do it for you as well. Better yet, you can do all three. Never limit yourself to only one option.

While social media marketing is a great tool, people still want that face to face personal connection. Even with social media marketing people still want some sort of connection outside of just a post or tweet. Many people use video, tele-conferences and pictures to try and give their audience a real feel for who they are, and this works for the most part, but it will never replace the real connection people feel when they can shake your hand or have that eye to eye contact with you.

So remember to use social media marketing as a tool along with making personal connections as much as possible.

PARTNERSHIPS

Partnerships are also a must. You cannot get far in the business world without other people. If you think you can do it all by yourself and make it to the top my friend, you are dead wrong!

Partnerships will open doors for you and your business that you cannot open alone. Finding the right partnerships is a big deal. You do not want to pair up with someone who will not benefit you. Just as you don't want someone to partner with you who you cannot help. It needs to be a win-win situation.

Finding the right partnerships may take some work and even a small investment at times, but it will be well worth it if you find the right people. Long term partnerships can be beneficial to your business.

You will need to have as many partners on board before launching your big event as possible. This is why your networking, and marketing are so very important.

Partnerships can also include virtual assistants. Not all of your partnerships have to be in your city or state. There are some great virtual assistants throughout the country and abroad that can help you accomplish tasks that need to be completed for your business.

Often virtual assistants can be hired at an affordable rate that will appeal to new business owners. Again, you'll want to do your research and find the right virtual assistant for your company and your needs.

Answer the following questions:

*How many quality partnerships do you have? If you have none, begin to reach out to people you would love to connect with.

_____
_____
_____
_____
_____

*How can I be of service to the partners I currently have?

_____
_____
_____

{Life Lesson}

Quality partnerships can completely change the dynamic of your business. Partnering with people who can add value to your business is such a big deal that you cannot afford to skip this step of the process.

Many times a partnership will assist you with getting more business or making more connections that would have been missed otherwise.

Partnerships also facilitate growth by allowing someone else to give you good advice, insight and knowledge on how to make your business better from a different perspective.

A good partnership works both ways and should always benefit all parties involved. You should never partner with a company or a person whom you feel will not benefit you or your company.

NOTICE TO EMPLOYER

Exit Strategy

If you are working a 9-5, now is the time to begin to say your goodbyes if you want to leave. Do it cheerfully and with gratitude. Keep in mind your 9-5 was a part of your journey and without it you would not be where you are today.

Not everyone who wants to start their own business will quit their day jobs before they are secure with their new business. Many people who want to start their own business are afraid of the uncertainty of not knowing how they will make money, how they will maintain the benefits of working a 9-5 such as insurance, 401k, and retirement funds. This is a normal response for someone who has always worked in the corporate world. I will admit it is difficult to think about the *how* when making a life changing decision that will affect you and your family.

What I have experienced and learned from the many entrepreneurs that I have read about, studied or worked with is that many of the successful entrepreneurs did not let the *how* of things keep them from moving forward. Most of them either had enough faith to make the change or their backs were up against the wall and they had no choice but to make things happen in order to survive.

My personal opinion is when you know, that you know, that you know that were you are is not where you are supposed to be, and God has a greater assignment awaiting you, you move past fear and jump right off the edge of the cliff with unshakable faith and move forward. This is where you have to be to be as a successful business owner and leader. You will not always know what is ahead of you, but you must move ahead anyway.

When you have a strong belief that you have a divine destiny assignment ahead of you, you know in your heart that you cannot afford to stay where you are.

Many people would stop being afraid to get up and live their dreams every day if they would just stop worrying about how things are going to get done and just make some moves. Believing in yourself and having the confidence to move from one level in your life to the next definitely takes faith in yourself and the process. So if you are lacking in faith do not just jump up and quit your job because you want to own your own business. Faith is what will sustain you when everything around you seems to be fighting against you. You must be strong in your ability to complete and finish your divine assignment without a doubt and despite the obstacles.

Keep It Simple & Sweet!

Example notice to your current employer:

Your Name
Your Address
Your City, State, Zip Code
Your Phone Number
Your Email

Date

Name

Title

Organization

Address

City, State, Zip Code

Dear Mr. / Ms. Last Name:

I am writing to announce my resignation from *Company Name*, effective *two weeks* from this date.
I've enjoyed working for you and managing a very successful team. Thank you for the opportunities for growth that you have provided me. I wish you and the company all the best. If I can be of any help during the transition, please don't hesitate to ask.

Sincerely,
Your Signature *(hard copy letter)*
Your Typed Name

*If you are planning to leave your 9-5 in 90 days do not regret making this decision. This is part of what is necessary for you to have a successful business of your own. Eventually, you will need all your time to be focused on your own company instead of 8 hours or more a day devoted to someone else's company. You will no longer be building someone else's dream because you are now building your own.

{Life Lesson}

As I mentioned earlier, some entrepreneurs are put into a situation where their back is up against the wall, and they have no other choice when starting to work for themselves.

While I had always wanted to own my own business, I never thought I would be forced into doing so when I did. I began to know that working a corporate job wasn't for me during the first year of my oldest son being born. He had so many problems and illnesses as a baby it was even hard to find childcare for him. As a college student and single mother, I had to find a way to make things happen for me and my son.

During his first year of life, we spent most of our days in the Children's Hospital and the E.R. I worked for just about every temp service in Oklahoma during this time along with many other jobs. I often had to quit jobs that were not understanding of my motherly responsibility and the fact that my son was sickly, and that I might be called to pick him up.

I gave up many career opportunities to be the very best mother I could be to my ill son. I committed to staying in school and often had to take day and night classes that would fit around the schedules of those who were helping me provide for my baby boy. Eventually, my grandmother found a childcare provider who was very supportive of me and who was willing to help me in every possible way. From the time my son began with the new childcare provider I started working harder on everything I wanted to succeed at in life. I did not waste one minute with the blessing I had been given. I went from 9-12 hours per semester to 12-15 hours per semester and working two jobs.

I was determined to use the gift God had blessed me with to turn things around for me and my son. There were still days I had to stay home with my son because of him not feeling well, but for the most part I was able to work harder than I ever had toward my dreams for our future.

LAUNCH EVENT

Exit Strategy

Your event is the most important part of the entire 90-day Exit Strategy. You have been working hard to get to this day. Your successful launch event. Give yourself at least 90 days to promote your big day. This event is your time to show the world who you are, how creative you are and why they must pay attention to you.

Your event is a big deal! So you will need time to plan. You will start by making a list of all of your connections you have made thus far from networking, marketing, partnerships and anybody who has supported you. You will then connect with your partners and discuss how and when you would like to have your launch event and how they may be able to support you in the event. Once you get your partners confirmed and a few other tasks, you are ready to start promoting your event. Ask your partners to assist you as well with promoting your event. It will benefit you both.

The most important thing during this phase is to enjoy every moment and have fun doing so. Don't let anything stop you now. You are fearless and unstoppable!

Answer the following:

What type of event are you planning? Ex. book launch, new business, launch party, etc.

_____

_____

_____

_____

Have you set a date for your event?

_____

_____

_____

Do you have the support you need to plan this event?

_____

_____

_____

_____

{Life Lesson}

Launching an event can be quite demanding of your time and energy. Be sure to work out all the details of the event on paper before putting everything together. This will help you stay organized and complete tasks in a timely fashion.

There are several tools you can use from the internet that will give you check list or to do list when preparing for particular events. You can always hire an event planner or assistant as well to manage this. Get the help you need to keep from getting overwhelmed.

I suggest that for your first event you keep things simple but informative. You do not want to have a huge event and people walk away not understanding the purpose. So make sure your event is more about the purpose than glamor. You'll have time for that later on down the line.

BUSINESS RESOURCES

Here are some of the most useful resources for first time business owners. There are many more, but I compiled a list of the top ones I used as a first-time business owner. Here they are:

www.Upwork.com
A site where you can hire virtual assistants to do anything from creating a bio to designing your website and doing daily tasks.

www.fiverr.com
A site where you can get almost any of your business needs completed for $5.00

www.Wordpress.com
A web hosting site that you control at all times with several different options and themes to choose from.

www.Hostgator.com
Provides hosting and domain services

www.GoDaddy.com
Provides hosting and domain services

www.Paypal.com
Payment processor services for personal and business owners. Everyone can get started with a free account.

www.Awebber.com
Provides Email marketing services

www.Picmonkey.com
Provides online photo editing services.

www.Hootesuite.com
Provides scheduling services and options for your social media accounts

www.freeconferencecall.com
Provides a free conference call number and set up to do conference calls and meetings online or by phone

www.Facebook.com
Free Social Media site

www.Twitter.com
Free Social Media site

www.LinkedIn.com
Free Business Social Media site

www.Meetup.com
Networking social site with many different groups to choose from in your area. You can even start your own networking group here.

CONCLUSION

Exit Strategy

My friend we have come to the end of your 90-day Exit Strategy together. Now is the time to celebrate the accomplishments you have made thus far. Go out and do something nice for yourself. You deserve it.

While this book is a basic guide to assisting anyone who wants to start their journey of becoming a business owner/entrepreneur, there will be many other things to learn along the way.

What I have shared with you here is years of basic experiences and knowledge I learned from my mentors, advisors and coaches along my journey. You can get any business started with just these few basic tools and lessons learned here.

Read this guide over and over again until the information becomes a ritual. You will use it in many different forms over your business journey. Start a collection of business and personal development reading materials. It will assist you and help you to recall certain things in time of need along the way. Reading will also help you learn more and more each and every time you pick up a new book. You will never get to a point when you know it all. So keep learning.

The most important thing I want you to know is that everything you need to be successful is already inside you. You must want success so bad that you will dig deep inside yourself to find what it is that will keep you motivated and determined to continue the journey.

I would love to assist you in any way that I can. Please visit my website for more information on strategy sessions, coaching opportunities, and other books that will help you accomplish your dreams no matter how big or small those dreams and desires may be.

You can always connect with me on the following sites:

www.laquitapoole.com
www.facebook.com/laquitathemaven
www.twitter.com/laquitathemaven

THANK YOU

I want to send my deepest gratitude to you for picking up this guide book and allowing me to assist you along your journey. Your divine assignment is so very important to this world and to who you are.

Many years ago when I first discovered I wanted to be an author and speaker, I struggled with how I would go about finding the courage to share my story and my experiences with the world. The more I began to learn who I was, my inner strength and divine assignment, I found peace in going forward.

While I have a great deal of experience, knowledge and life lessons deep inside of me, I know it means nothing to be a survivor of anything if you don't share those experiences with someone who can be helped by it.

I have come a long way. I still have a long way to go. As I continue my journey, I want to be of service to those who believe in me and my passion to keep pushing when everything else seems to be pushing back. I know what it's like to be starting out with no money, a mountain of debt, lack of knowledge or skills and so many other obstacles. However, I also know what it is like to get over it, and hold on to the promise that we are meant to live out our dreams and live a full life right here on this earth.

My personal advice to you is never give up until you have completed your divine assignment. There is nothing in this world holding you back but you. Everything you need to complete your journey is already inside of you.

You may have to step outside your comfort zone, but this is good. Being uncomfortable is how great success is accomplished. You are not perfect, and you are going to make mistakes along the way. You want this to happen because it is the only way to learn and keep growing.

Don't look for approval. God approved you when he gave you the dream and the divine assignment that only you can accomplish.

I would love to hear your thoughts on the book and would so appreciate a quick review.

LaQuita Lewis-Poole
WWW.LAQUITAPOOLE.COM
INFO@LAQUITAPOOLE.COM

BONUSES

Motivational Tips:

1.   Clear your mind of all the clutter and negative things in and around your life. Time for a new start.

2.   Make up in your mind you will get rid of the old way of thinking. You are starting a new mindset right now.

3.   Agree only to think positively and be positive starting right now. It will change your life.

4.   Set new goals, accomplish your dreams and then dream bigger. Always dream big!

5.   Go out and meet new friends and hang out with new groups. You need to align yourself with people who are where you are trying to go.

6.   Do something challenging every day that will stimulate your mind and/or body. You need new experiences.

7.   Face your fears daily one step at a time. You will be shocked at what is hidden inside of you.

8.   LAUGH. LAUGH. LAUGH. Go to a comedy show. Watch some funny movies. Find something so funny that you will get a deep, soul reaching laugh from. This will relieve stress.

9.   Smile. No matter how bad you think things are they are really not that bad. If you are living, you should be smiling. Smile about life!

10. Be grateful! Every moment you are given on this earth is a blessing. Someone somewhere was not able to see this day. Be grateful for life and use it to the fullest.

SAMPLE AFFIRMATIONS

I am whole, strong and powerful in all that I do.

I am grateful to be alive.

Faith:

I have the faith that everything I want to achieve is possible.

All good things are coming to me now.

Forgiveness:

I forgive anyone who has come into my life and hurt me.

I let go of all anger, fear, and hurt.

I forgive myself.

Confidence:

I am a confident woman/man.

I am free to be me.

Happiness:

I see the beauty in all things around me each day.

I take time to laugh and enjoy life every day.

Money:

I have the power to manifest the money that is on purpose for me now.

Money is being made just for me right now.

I have more than enough.

Love:

I feel the love and joy in my life daily.

I give and receive love every day.

Exit Strategy

ABOUT THE AUTHOR

For the past fifteen years, Professional Life Coach and author LaQuita Lewis-Poole, has mentored men, women and families in need. Her newest book, *Exit Strategy*, is the culmination of her experience and chronicles her own remarkable business journey. She is also the author of Break the Money Curse and the *Life Lessons* Guide and the CEO of LSL Media & Publishing and LSLP Global Empowerment.

LaQuita's success didn't happen overnight. Like many in our society, she lived through some of the worst life has to offer. Yet she overcame, flourished, and as a Professional Life Coach & Youth and Family coach, inspires others to realize their dreams. Whether they need gentle direction or tough love, she has been there to help them get on their feet so they could return to school, break bad habits, create realistic life plans and start businesses, along with much more.

In addition to her private coaching practice, LaQuita is a contracted Case Manager & Behavioral Health Rehabilitation Specialist for the state of Oklahoma. She has worked extensively with at-risk individuals, in many capacities, and was previously the President of Teen Mothers Second Chance, the President of the Teen Resource Center and the CEO of Making an Impact Counseling Services.

She understands how overwhelming circumstances can be. She knows the odds are sometimes stacked against us. However, she's living proof that any goal can be achieved if you are determined to succeed. LaQuita's greatest passion is helping her clients see their worth and become the very best they can be. Her vibrant personality and positive outlook, combined with her education and expertise, has made her a professional life coach who helps her clients grow to their fullest potentials.

LaQuita currently lives in Texas. She is the mother of two sons, a beautiful daughter and is married to her best friend. She always says that her life is phenomenal.

LaQuita Sharee Lewis-Poole

www.ingramcontent.com/pod-product-compliance
Lightning Source LLC
Chambersburg PA
CBHW072207090426
42740CB00012B/2430